Sam's Trip and Slip

'Chirp, Chirp, Chirpity, Chirp.' Cornelius listened to the birdsong as he walked home from his night shift; his night manager had taken his warning light off his head, making him feel a lot lighter!

He found the night shift tough and long, but it was good to help his colleagues warn motorists of the dangers while there were roadworks. Now he was ready for his bed and getting all snuggly and warm. He debated whether to have a cooked breakfast of egg and sausage or just some cereal. Decisions, decisions.

As he continued along the street, he could see Pete, the local postman.

'Hello Pete, you're early today; I see you have your trolley.'

'Hello Cornelius, yes, I managed to get out early; the trolley is perfect for the weight we have to carry.'

'Well, it's good that you take care of your back Pete'.

'While you are here, Cornelius, did you know the crocodile can grow up to sixteen feet?'

'Wow, that is amazing, Pete.' said Cornelius.

'Yes, but I have only seen a crocodile with four feet.'

'Ha, ha, that was very funny, oh, is that the time? I must be getting on; I need to get home for breakfast, then sleep; I have another shift tonight; see you next time.'

'See you later, Cornelius.

Looking up the road, he could see a school crossing – Aha, he thought, there's the lovely Dora, the lollipop lady with Lily lollipop, they always do such a great job, carefully guiding children safely across the road to and from School.

'Hello, Dora and Lily!' he called out.

'Oh, hello Cornelius, how are you?'

'Just tired after a long night shift!' he yawned loudly. 'Just started working, have you?' he asked them.

'Yes, that's right.' Dora replied.

A row of tiny cones arrived to cross the road, all holding hands, wearing their high visibility jackets for safety; they were going to Cone School.

Remembering when he had attended Cone school many years ago, Cornelius was grateful for the training he had received. It had stood him in good stead for the job he loved.

'Sorry Cornelius, I can't stop to talk; I just got to get these little ones across the road.' Lily gave Cornelius a friendly little wink.

'No problem.' Cornelius replied as he made his way past.

The tiny Cones were chatting and giggling as they safely crossed the road guided by Dora and Lily.

They turned round to thank Dora and Lily, then walked through the school gates.

On his way, he noted a young man walking on the other side of the road; he was wearing large white headphones and had his head down, looking at his phone.

Oh, dear, Cornelius thought to himself, now there's an accident waiting to happen! He's not watching where he's going and cannot hear anything around him with those headphones; what if he falls down a pothole or crosses the road in front of the heavy traffic!

No sooner had this thought crossed his mind, he heard a screech of tyres!!!!!! The young man had fallen down an unattended pothole!!! Cornelius could see a pair of legs sticking out of the hole.

The traffic had come to a slow crawl as people wanted to see what had happened.

Cornelius ran over to the young man and peered down the hole.

'Hello,' he called out… 'Are you okay? What's your name? Are you hurt?' asked Cornelius.

The young man replied, 'Er…yeah, I'm okay, thanks; I just feel a bit silly; my name's Sam.'

'I'm Cornelius. Could you give me your hand? I will pull you out.'

By this time, other people had come to help, and together, they pulled him out.

Sam looked a bit sheepish as he sat next to the pothole.

He sat up and thanked everyone for their help.

'Thank you ever so much! Phew, I didn't see that coming!'

Cornelius wondered if the hole was reported, it was a massive hole and could have caused a lot of damage to a car, motorbike, or bicycle.

A few moments later, a Highway maintenance truck arrived with two workers to repair the pothole.

Cornelius waved at the cones in the back of the truck; some of them had worked with him before, and the workers made sure they had enough cones to watch over the hole.

After checking that Sam was alright, Cornelius made his way back home.

Phew! I'm so pleased he didn't hurt himself, thought Cornelius; it could have been very nasty for him, but he wasn't watching where he was walking.

As Cornelius continued, he stopped outside the Supermarket and wondered how Tricia Trolley was getting on; he missed seeing her but thought he should head home.

In the Supermarket, Wet Floor was getting ready for his shift; he had an essential job. When an announcement was made, for example, - 'BING BONG!!!!' - 'Spillage in aisle fifteen – next to the baked beans,' he was to report to the spillage immediately to prevent anyone slipping up.

He loved his job and was very diligent. He was proud to have such a responsible position. He always did his utmost to attend to the spillages. To have anyone slip up in the Supermarket would be very serious indeed.

However, today, Wet Floor was not feeling his best; he thought he was coming down with a cold; he felt sluggish and had a niggling headache.

'Oh well,' he said to himself, 'I will have to do the best I can.'

He had a little walk down each aisle, looking for potential hazards.

It also gave him ideas about what he could have for tea that night. He could see where the special offers were and when he could, he would make his way there and see if he could pick up a bargain while on his break.

'Mmmm,' he said to himself, 'I fancy sausage and beans for tea.'

He could see Carrie chatting to Polly, the two reusable shopping bags often seen in the Supermarket.

Seeing that they were busy talking, he walked down the aisle, looking at the bargains.

He came across Tricia Trolley; Wet Floor had not seen her in the Supermarket for some time, so he felt this was an excellent chance to catch up with her.

'Hello, Tricia, lovely to see you again; how are you doing?'

'Not too bad, thank you, Wet Floor, ' replied Tricia.

'Any spillages?' she enquired.

'Nah, nothing, bit quiet really,' he raised his eyes upward.

Wet Floor became so engrossed in conversation and telling jokes to Tricia that he didn't hear the tannoy:

'BING BONG!!!!'

In a shrill voice, a lady announced: 'Spillage in aisle eight next to the frozen chickens, Wet Floor to attend immediately!'

Again, Wet Floor hadn't heard the announcement as he and Tricia were giggling about another incident concerning a packet of fish fingers the previous day.

'BING BONG!!!!!!!!!'

This time the lady's announcement over the tannoy was thunderously loud!

'Spillage in aisle eight! Would Wet Floor attend immediately, please!!!!!!'

Wet Floor finally heard the lady, and with a quick cheerio to Tricia, he made his way to aisle eight.

Wet Floor ran as fast as he could.

By the time he got to the aisle, to his great dismay, he could see a young man sprawled across the Floor, the headphones he had been wearing had slid off, and a baked bean tin crushed his phone; the young man had slipped up on the spillage! Disaster!

'Oh, no!' shouted Wet Floor. Gasping for breath, he reached the young man.

'Are you okay? Are you hurt?' he asked the young man.

'Oh, Man! It's not my day!' the young man replied.

'I am so sorry; I should have got to the spillage sooner, but, I, er, um, oh dear….am so sorry! I was um, er, um, chatting to someone. I got a bit distracted; I can only apologise!' said Wet Floor.

'It's alright, mate,' said the young man, 'I'm not hurt; I feel a bit silly; it's the second time I've had an accident today.'

'Are you sure you're not hurt? I am truly sorry.' Wet Floor was very sad as he felt he could have prevented this from happening.

'Don't worry, mate; I'm okay.'

The young man picked himself up and gathered up his headphones and phone.

'Oh no, my phone's broken!' cried the young man.

'Why don't I show you where we sell our phones here? Perhaps I can get a discount for you as you have been so understanding?'

'That would be great, thanks, matey!' said the young man.

'My name's Wet Floor; let me attend to this mess, then we will be on our way.'

'Okay, my name's Sam; I'm in no hurry.'

After clearing the spillage, Wet Floor took Sam to the phone display.

Sam chose a new phone, then proceeded to the checkout with Wet Floor, who kept his word and got him a good deal, this made Sam very happy, and he promised to be more careful in the future.

Wet Floor was glad that things turned out okay in the end.

It was time for his break; he decided to get some fruit for his cold.

Hmm, Oranges have a lot of vitamin C; that will be what I need; I'd better get some tissues as well, Wet Floor thought to himself.

Wet Floor grabbed a paper bag for the Oranges, picked up a box of tissues, and then headed off to the checkout.

When he arrived at the checkout, he could see 'Charlie', better known as 'Checkout Charlie.'

Charlie has been working at the Supermarket for many years; his dream is to be an employee of the year; he is often helpful to staff and customers.

'BEEP BOP!'

'Hello Wet Floor, not feeling well? Asked Charlie.

'Hello Charlie, I will be fine, just a bit of a cold, I dink, Oranges have a lot of vitamin C, and dis box of dissues will help my dose.'

'BEEP BOP!'

'Yes, said Charlie, I see your nose is a bit red.'

'I have to get back; my break is nearly over; see you later,' sniffed Wet Floor.

Even though Wet Floor had a cold, he was more worried about what could have happened if Sam had been hurt.

Wet Floor came to the end of his shift; he headed home after gathering his belongings.

On his way home, he met Postman Pete.

'Hello Pete, said Wet Floor, 'you're late today.'

'Hello Wet Floor, yes, it has been quite a day. Did you know the Crocodile can grow up to…….'

Wet Floor interrupted Pete.

'Sorry, Pete, I have to get home, my dose is very sore, watch out… I'm about to sneeze!!!!'

'AHHHHHHHHHHHHH………..

'CHOOOOOOOOOOOOOOO!!!!!!!!!'

It was too late for Wet Floor to reach for his tissues; the force from the sneeze had blown all the letters out of Pete's hand, nearly sending him off his feet.

Pete quickly gathered up the letters that had blown out of his hands.

'That's okay Wet Floor; I understand; I will save the story for another day; get well soon.'

Wet Floor sniffed, blew his nose and said, 'Bye Pete, keep up the good work.'

See you in the next book.

To my wife Sarah for her contribution and my inspiration.

Printed by BoD in Norderstedt, Germany

9 781739 691417